THE HISTORY OF OPTARE

KEITH A. JENKINSON

AMBERLEY

First published 2020

Amberley Publishing
The Hill, Stroud
Gloucestershire, GL5 4EP

www.amberley-books.com

Copyright © Keith A. Jenkinson, 2020

The right of Keith A. Jenkinson to be identified
as the Author of this work has been asserted
in accordance with the Copyright, Designs and
Patents Act 1988.

ISBN 978 1 4456 9694 2 (print)
ISBN 978 1 4456 9695 9 (ebook)

British Library Cataloguing in Publication Data.
A catalogue record for this book is available from
the British Library.

Typesetting by Aura Technology and Software
Services, India. Printed in the UK.

Introduction

Following the closure, by Leyland Vehicles, of bus bodybuilders Chas H. Roe, in September 1984, its Crossgates, Leeds, factory then remained empty until February 1985 when Russell Richardson, a former Roe director, backed by the West Yorkshire Enterprise Board and a number of former Roe employees, formed a new company, Optare, to purchase the plant and restart coachbuilding there.

After commencing its activities, the newly formed company set about designing, and building, a midibus body mounted on a Dennis Domino chassis, and gained an order for fourteen of these little buses from South Yorkshire PTE, the first of which was delivered in July 1985. Then, in October 1985, came ten double-deckers on Leyland Olympian chassis for West Yorkshire PTE, of which five were given coach seats and two were built as convertible open-toppers. All were built to the final Roe design fitted to 151 of the PTE's Olympians between 1981 and 1984, the last few of which were completed by ECW at Lowestoft.

Having now settled in to its new role as an independent coachbuilder, in 1986 Optare began to create more of its own designs and, in addition to building fifteen midibus bodies on Leyland Cub chassis for West Yorkshire PTE, similar to those on South Yorkshire PTE's Dennis Domino chassis, it launched a completely new twenty-five-seat body constructed on the VW LT55 chassis, designating it the CityPacer. This featured a steeply raked front with a large, single-piece windscreen with triangular quarter lights, and immediately attracted interest from London Buses, who purchased fifty-two, the delivery of which commenced in July 1986 and was completed in February 1987. Numerous other CityPacers were built for municipal and independent operators with some being coach-seated and marketed as the InterCityPacer, and others having a wheelchair lift fitted in their rear bulkhead for local authority use. In addition, two CityPacers were built to left-hand drive format, fitted with coach seats, and purchased in October 1987 by Dutch operator NZH, to become the first Optare products to be sold overseas.

Optare was also busy in 1986, converting Freight Rover 350D vans to form sixteen-seat minibuses and minicoaches. Fifteen of these were supplied to Yorkshire Rider, while the remaining twenty-five were purchased by independent operators, most of whom opted for the coach-seated version. Also in 1986/7, Optare adapted twelve Dodge S56s to become eight-seat social services buses for Leeds City Council, and followed these in 1987 with thirty-nine Renault Master vans, which were transformed into eight-seat minibuses with wheelchair lifts for the Northern Region Health Authority and Cleveland Ambulance Service. In the meantime, in 1986 Optare broke from tradition by surprisingly building two vans on Ford R1115 chassis for Leeds City Council.

Double deck production restarted in February 1987 when five coach-seated examples were built for Yorkshire Rider. Then, in February 1988, Cambus bought three, and Maidstone Boro'line took the first of its order for fourteen, although two of them were diverted to London independent Cityrama before delivery. Following these, between April and October 1988, were ten for Reading Buses, three of which were coach-seated and seven were of two-door layout. All the above mentioned were built to the old Roe design and were mounted on Leyland Olympian chassis, with the last to be built being one of Maidstone's examples which was delayed until June 1989. These proved to be the last double-deckers to be built by Optare until 2008, as will be seen later.

Following the success of the CityPacer, of which 294 were built, the last in August 1989 except for one in April 1992, and quickly seeing the need for a larger midibus, in August 1987 Optare launched the StarRider, which was constructed on a Mercedes Benz 811D chassis. Having a steeply raked front similar to the CityPacer, it had a shallower one-piece flat windscreen and could accommodate between twenty-six and thirty-three bus or coach seats. Purchased by major operators such as Badgerline, London Buses, and Yorkshire Traction, the StarRider also proved popular with independent companies in both bus and coach format, and 240 were built before production came to an end in August 1989. Meanwhile, in a bid to break into the Sri Lankan market, in 1987 Optare joined forces with Japanese technology company Itochu and Sri Lankan automobile manufacturer Ceymo to jointly build a semi-integral midibus based on the StarRider, which it named 'ColumboRider'. Despite a sizeable number being produced, Optare found that the ColumboRider proved too expensive to build and thus discontinued it in favour of an export version of the MetroRider.

Optare's first venture into the full-size single-deck bus market came in September 1988 when it introduced the step-entrance Delta, which was based on the DAF SB220 chassis. Using a bolted aluminium body frame licensed from Alusuisse, it featured a raked front with a one-piece curved, wrap-round windscreen, and was offered in single and dual-door configuration. Although production largely ceased in 1993, the Delta remained available until 1999, with the last example being purchased by Birmingham independent Claribels in June of that year. A total of 369 Deltas were built.

Upon the closure of bus manufacturer MCW in May 1989, Optare purchased the rights to build the integrally constructed Metrorider mini/midibus and also, jointly with Dutch chassis manufacturer DAF, bought the rights for the integral double-deck MCW Metrobus. After transferring the tooling from MCW's factory in Birmingham to its Crossgates, Leeds, plant, Optare began building the mini/midibus, which it renamed 'MetroRider', in November 1989 and offered it in varying lengths to accommodate between twenty-three and thirty-three seats. Proving to be an extremely popular model, the MetroRider remained in production until April 2000, during which time 1,159 had been built. Of these, four were electric-powered eighteen-seaters, new in November 1993, and two were twenty-nine seaters propelled by compressed natural gas and placed in service in June 1996.

Having seen Dennis introduce its Dart midibus in 1989, in April 1991 Optare took the decision to build a similar sized step-entrance bus on a MAN 11.190 chassis and named it the 'Vecta'. With seating for forty-one/forty-two passengers, it used much of the same design as the Delta but had a more upright front profile with a one-piece windscreen, and was largely purchased by major, rather than independent, operators. It continued to be available until August 1997 when the last of the 130 built entered service with Tillingbourne at Cranleigh.

Following their joint purchase of the MCW Metrobus, DAF and Optare developed a new double-decker named the 'Spectra' using an Optare body on a DAF DB250 chassis. Incorporating much of the design used on the Vecta, the new double-decker, which was described as 'partly low-floor', made its debut in January 1992. Originally in step entrance format, it continued in production until February 1995, by which time 115 had been built. Then, after a three-year gap, in January 1998 the Spectra was relaunched as a full low-floor bus and remained in production until March 2003, although a further two were built in 2004 and the final two were completed in 2006. Although most Spectras were built with a single door, thirty-seven were of two-door format, with thirty-one of these being exported to Izmir, and Istanbul, Turkey, in left-hand drive configuration. A total of 151 low-floor examples were built and, as a result of its collaboration with DAF, all Spectra bodies were constructed on DAF DB250 chassis.

In an attempt towards further expansion, in May 1990 Optare became part of the Dutch company United Bus, which had been formed when DAF Bus was split from DAF NV which had traded as Leyland DAF in the UK. Although this gave Optare a stronger presence in the European bus market, various difficulties caused United Bus to collapse in February 1993, soon after which Optare returned to independent status when it was repurchased by its management. During its time within United Bus, and for several years beyond, Optare acted as the UK agent for DAF's Bova Futura coaches and provided parts and maintenance for them in addition to negotiating sales.

Its return to private ownership resulted in Optare turning to manufacturers other than DAF to supply it with chassis and, in May 1994, launched its Sigma model, which used a Dennis Lance chassis. Design-wise, the Sigma was basically a longer version of the Vecta, and fifty-four were built, all but three of which were purchased by Brighton & Hove, Go-Ahead Northern (Gateshead), and Trent, with the final example entering service in May 1996. All were built in single-door format except for one for Ipswich which was dual-door. Then, in March 1995, Optare began building bodies on the Mercedes Benz 0405 chassis. Given the name 'Prisma', these again were very similar in appearance to the Sigma and Vecta, except that they incorporated a standard Mercedes Benz 0405 front. The Prisma remained in production until December 1998, by which time 122 had been built.

The next new model to appear from the Optare factory was the Excel, an integrally constructed low-floor single-decker which was available in single- or dual-door format and made its debut in November 1995. Incorporating much of Optare's established design, albeit with a curved front and deep one-piece windscreen, it was offered in five different lengths – 9.6m, 10.0m, 10.7m, 11.5m and 11.8m – with seating ranging between twenty-seven and forty-five passengers. The Excel was available with either a Cummins or Mercedes Benz engine, and a total of 590 were built at Optare's Crossgates factory, with production ending in September 2004.

Seeking to expand again, in 1996 Optare purchased Autobus Classique, a coachbuilding company at Hellaby, South Yorkshire, who produced a small range of mini/midicoaches, almost exclusively on Mercedes Benz chassis. At the time of its takeover, Autobus Classique's most popular model was the Nouvelle, which Optare upgraded as the 'Nouvelle 2', and which bore some frontal resemblance to its StarRider. Additionally, however, Autobus Classique also built some mini/midibuses based on van conversions: one, a Mercedes Benz sixteen-seater, sold as the 'Super Sprinter 16'; the other was a twenty-four-seater given the name 'Mercedes Benz Vario 24'. All production ceased in July 2009, after which the Hellaby plant continued in use as an Optare sales and service centre.

During 1997, Optare further expanded its portfolio when it entered into an agreement with Spanish midicoach builder Ferqui SL to sell its Solera model in the UK as the 'Optare Solera'. Initially, two variants were offered, both mounted on a Mercedes Benz Atego chassis, with the Solera having its entrance door behind the front axle and the SoleraHD having it forward of the front axle. Following these, in October 2005, from Ferqui SL came the 'Toro' mounted on a Mercedes Benz 0815D/0816D chassis, and the 'Soroco' midicoach which initially used a Mercedes Benz CDi Sprinter chassis and then a Mercedes Benz 515CDi underframe. These were followed, in 2009, by the 'Viedo' on an Iveco Daily chassis, and the Rapido, based on the Fiat Ducato and Isuzu, all of which carried Optare branding. After fifteen years of co-operation, Optare ended its association with Ferqui SL in January 2012.

Having produced the MetroRider since its acquisition in 1989 from MCW, in May 1998 Optare launched its successor, a low-floor model given the name 'Solo', which was derived from it being 'so low'. With a body largely replicating the conventionally sized Excel, with its curved front and large single-piece windscreen, but featuring a more pronounced curve, the Solo was originally offered in 8.5m and 9.2m lengths and was fitted with a Mercedes Benz engine. In 2004, however, 7.8m, 8.8m, 9.5m, 9.9m and 10.2m lengths were added, with some of the shorter models also being offered from November 2004 as the 'Slim Line', the shorter models having a narrower width to make them more suitable for rural services with narrow roads. Additionally, Cummins engines were also offered as an alternative to the Mercedes Benz unit. Then, looking to the future, in July 2011 Optare introduced a hybrid version of the Solo, following this with an electric variant in June 2012. The only UK solos not built to single front-door configuration were two supplied to MacMillan Cancer Support with a centre entrance for use as promotional vehicles, and nine dual-door examples purchased by CT Plus, Hackney, in 2012. By the time right-hand drive Solo production came to an end in September 2012, a total of 3,843 had been built (of which four were exported to New Zealand in 2008 and ten were supplied to Arriva in Malta in 2011). In addition to these, seventy left-hand drive examples had also been constructed, in single and dual-door format, between May 2002 and January 2012, for operation in Denmark, Sweden, Holland, Germany, and Israel.

In the meantime, Optare had once again changed ownership when, in 2000, it was purchased for £21.5m by Hungarian-owned North American Bus Industries (NABI), which was based in part of the massive former Ikarus factory on the outskirts of Budapest. This gave Optare a platform for its products in the North American and Hungarian markets with its badge engineered Solo and Excel models, the latter, however, using a Scania L94UB chassis and marketed as the NABI 700SE. Only thirteen NABI 700SEs were built, all at the company's Kaposvar factory, in dual- or triple-door format for Hungarian operators, while the NABI 30-LFN (Solo) was constructed at Budapest, from where all the 173 produced in 2001/2 crossed the water to the USA. Meanwhile, in addition to its two Optare models, NABI was also developing the CompoBus, an integral two-axle single-decker constructed in fibre-reinforced composite material, which could be powered by CNG or diesel, or built as a diesel-electric hybrid. For CompoBus production, in 2002 NABI built a new factory in Kaposvar, Hungary, where the 700SE was also constructed, while other models built for the North American market remained at Budapest. Then, after NABI found itself in financial difficulties in 2005, Optare severed its ties with its Hungarian owner, and was re-purchased by its UK management for £11.8m, thus returning to independence (again!).

On the small vehicle front, in September 2000, soon after it was acquired by NABI, Optare, in the UK, launched a new low floor, integrally composite-constructed minibus, naming it the 'Alero'. Of 7.2m length, 2.0m width, and 2.5m height, it featured a steeply curved front, seating for twelve to sixteen passenger, dependent on a wheelchair space, a wide entrance through which two passengers could board side by side, and, optionally, a destination box mounted on its front roof dome. Powered by a 2.8 litre, 4-cylinder Iveco engine, it was available with manual or automatic transmission, featured air conditioning and climate control, and continued in production, at Optare's Hellaby factory, until December 2008, by which time 312 had been built.

Back in the UK, in September 2002 Optare entered into an agreement with Irisbus to finish the bodies of its Agora Lines model, a 12m low-floor city bus that had originally been built by Renault, and later by Irisbus and Karosa, on mainland Europe since 1995. Despite proving popular in Europe, the Agora Line largely failed to attract UK customers and, although it remained available until May 2007, only twenty-three were shipped from Annalay (France) for completion at Crossgates.

Also in 2002, Optare entered into partnership with Dutch coachbuilder Plastisol, who produced a glass-fibre reinforced polyester-bodied minicoach named 'Bonito', based on the Ford Transit and later, in 2012, on the Fiat Ducato chassis. However, after failing to gain a single sale for the Bonito in the UK, Optare ended its association with Plastisol in 2014.

In the meantime, Optare had set up an after sales service division, under the name Unitec, from premises at Thurrock and the Autobus Classique factory at Hellaby and, in 2009, renamed this Optare Product Support, and continued from the Thurrock site and part of the Hellaby plant, following its closure in 2012.

Shortly before leaving NABI, in October 2004 Optare introduced a new integrally constructed low-floor single-decker that was conventionally sized, and which was built in the UK at Crossgates and given the name 'Tempo'. Initially powered by a Mercedes Benz engine, and later offered with a MAN unit, it had an upright frontal appearance with a deep windscreen and was available in 10.6m, 11.3m, and 12m lengths. With the exception of those operated by Stagecoach East London, Metroline, London United, and Manchester Airport, who opted for dual-door configuration, all the others were built in single-door format. Never proving as popular as Optare had hoped, production of the Tempo, which had been updated in 2011 with a curved front and designated the 'TempoSR', ceased in December of the following year except for fifteen which were supplied to Australian customers between August 2014 and December 2017, and four that were purchased by Manchester Airport in May 2017. In total, 239 were built, plus a solitary left-hand drive variant that was constructed in October 2007 and demonstrated in Germany, Denmark and Holland, but sadly attracted no orders.

Then, in June 2007 Optare introduced a new low-floor midibus which was given the name 'Versa'. With a stylish curved front, and a roof line which was swept up at the front and sloped downwards midway along its body, its destination indicator was mounted on the front roof dome. Powered by a Mercedes Benz engine, it was offered in six different lengths from 9.7m to 11.7m and was available in both single and dual-door format. In 2010, a hybrid variant, with a battery pod mounted on the rear part of its roof, was added to the range and then, in 2012, an electric version made its debut. By December 2018, a total of 881 had been built, with production continuing throughout 2019. From 2013, the Versa was also offered in left-hand drive, single- and dual-door format, with either diesel or electric propulsion, with thirty-nine being built for operation in Sweden, Switzerland, Aberbaijan, and Bahrain.

Following hot on the heels of the Versa, and despite the Solo still being in full production, in September 2007 Optare launched a revised version of the latter, designated 'SoloSR', which style-wise was a scaled down version of the Versa but featured a glazed front roof dome behind which its destination screen was positioned. Offered in a range of different lengths from 7.1m to 9.95m, and in conventional and slim line widths, it could be powered by a Mercedes Benz or Cummins engine, and was also available as an electric or hybrid vehicle. All the Optare SoloSRs built to date are of single-door layout, except for eight purchased in 2012 by Richmond's, Epsom, for use in London, and a number exported to Australia. Of the 1,536 SoloSRs built up to February 2019, 221 have been sold to overseas customers in Australia/New Zealand, Hong Kong, Jersey, Cape Town, South Africa, and Malta.

On 14 March 2008, Optare changed ownership yet again when it was purchased by Jamesstan Investments, a company controlled by the Darwen Group's chairman, Ron Stanley. Although Optare remained an independent company, after a reverse takeover by the smaller Darwen Group was completed in July 2008, this additionally gave it control of Blackburn-based East Lancashire Coachbuilders whose single-deck Esteem, and double-deck Olympus models were then rebranded as Optare products.

Having been introduced by East Lancs in September 2006, after the company's acquisition by Optare only forty-six Esteem bodies were built – six single-door examples on Volvo B7RLE chassis for Kent County Council, and forty dual-door examples on Alexander Dennis Enviro200 chassis for London General – before it was discontinued in July 2009. The Olympus, however, remained in production at Blackburn, under the Optare name, until June 2011, during which time 138 were built, some single-door, others dual-door, on ADL Trident, Scania N230UD and Volvo B9TL chassis in two- or three-axle configurations. In addition, an open or part open-top version was produced under the name 'Visionaire' with seventy-one being built, nine of which were for Maltese customers. Also built was the OmniDekka, introduced by East Lancs in 2001 on the DAF DB250, Volvo B7TL, Dennis Trident and Scania N230UD and N270UD chassis which, after the Optare takeover, was only supplied to Nottingham City Transport who purchased eighty-five, the last of which was placed in service in November 2011.

Soon after taking over East Lancashire Coachbuilders, Optare launched two new models, one being a new version of its Solo model, named the 'Solo+', the other a double-decker designated the 'Rapta'. The Solo+ lacked any of the styling of the SoloSR, with slab-shaped sides and front and a flat roof, while the Rapta, powered by a MAN EuroV engine, was a dual-door model promoted as being available in 10m and 11.9m lengths. Although both made their debut at the Euro Bus Expo at the NEC, Birmingham, in October 2008, neither was favourably received by operators and they were abandoned before entering production. Two Solo+s had been built, both of which were rebuilt as standard SoloSRs, while the solitary Rapta was quietly dismantled without being completed.

Then, in 2009, as part of its rationalisation programme, Optare closed its former Autobus Classique factory at Hellaby, and, two years later, in October 2011, opened a new state-of-the-art facility at Sherburn-in-Elmet, North Yorkshire, closing its original Crossgates, Leeds, plant in the process. Following this, it also closed its East Lancashire Coachbuilders at Blackburn in May 2012, thus leaving all its production based at one site. Meanwhile, a milestone was reached when, in 2012, Optare built its 10,000th vehicle.

During this time, Indian bus and coach manufacturer Ashok Leyland acquired a 26 per cent stake in Optare, increasing this to 75 per cent in December 2011, and then 99.08 per cent in 2018, thus gaining full control of the company.

Having taken the decision to cease building bodies on other manufacturers' chassis and only undertake construction of integral buses, Optare designed a new lightweight double-deck model named the 'Metrodecker' and built a prototype in December 2012. Offered with either a Mercedes Benz Euro6 engine or as a fully electric vehicle, it was to be available in 10.5m or 11.14m length in single- or dual-door configuration. It was, however, not until November 2015 that a second prototype made its debut, followed by two more in April 2016 and June 2018, with full production finally commencing in 2019, orders having been gained for five diesel-powered examples for Reading Buses and electric versions for Metroline, London (thirty-one), and First York (twenty-one).

Finally, in November 2013 Optare launched the 'MetroCity', a new low-weight integral single-decker, initially for the London bus market, which bore a close resemblance to the Versa. Later offered nationally, it was offered with a choice of 9.9m, 10.10m, 10.6m, 10.8m, and 11.52m lengths. It was powered by a Mercedes Benz Euro6 engine and was available in single- or dual-door format, while in July 2014 an electric version of the MetroCity was added, designated the MetroCityEV. By March 2019, a total of 274 MetroCitys had been built, of which 116 were 11.52m examples supplied to two New Zealand operators.

Over the years, Optare has given names to its different models, such as the Delta, Spectra and Solo etc., and has used a system of numeric coding to signify overall vehicle lengths – e.g. the Excel L1070 has a 10.7m overall length, the Excel L1150 is 11.5m long and the Solo M850 is 8.5m long. In addition, suffixes have been added to the numeric codes to indicate the model's width or propulsion on non-standard models, e.g. SL for slim line (narrower width), H for hydrogen propulsion, or EV for electric vehicles, etc.

After weathering a number of turbulent times during its thirty-five-year history, and enduring a number of changes in ownership, Optare has nevertheless survived to retain its position as a major UK bus manufacturer, and throughout the years has produced several innovative models, thus proving that small acorns can still grow into large oaks.

Without the help of several friends and fellow enthusiasts, the photographic content of this book would have a number of gaps and thus I extend my thanks to all those, credited within the captions, who have generously allowed me to use their work. Unfortunately, however, I have been unable to trace some of the photographers, and thus I sincerely apologise for being unable to name them and hope that they will forgive me, but will, however, enjoy seeing their work in print, for without them this book would have been much less comprehensive.

Where it all began. Optare's original factory at Crossgates, Leeds, which had previously been Chas H. Roe's headquarters and production facility. (Author's collection)

Showing the curved-top windscreens fitted by Roe to its Leyland Olympians supplied to London Country and Bristol Omnibus, London Country LR48 (A148 FPG) is seen here at Brighton while undertaking a seaside excursion in 1986. (K. A. Jenkinson)

Amongst the last bodies to be built by Chas H. Roe before its closure in 1984 was that fitted to West Yorkshire PTE's Leyland Olympian 5116 (A116 KUM), seen here in its Yorkshire Rider days, in August 1990, approaching Bradford transport interchange. (K. A. Jenkinson)

The first bodies built by Optare were fourteen midibuses on Dennis Domino chassis for South Yorkshire PTE in July–September 1985. Here, 54 (C54 HDT) is seen at Bradford Interchange on 17 September 1987. It is operating the city's free Shop Hopper service while on loan to Yorkshire Rider, whose fleet name has been added to its rightful owner's Nipper livery. (K. A. Jenkinson)

Awaiting its passengers in Stockport bus station in 1991, Stevenson of Spath's ex-South Yorkshire Optare-bodied Dennis Domino 223 (C42 HDT), which was new in September 1985, wears the local Pacer fleet name of its new owner. (Author's collection)

Optare's first double-deck bodies were supplied to West Yorkshire PTE on Leyland Olympian chassis between October and December 1985. Built to the former Roe design, pictured in Bradford Interchange and branded for the White Rose Express service to Sheffield, is Gold Rider-liveried coach-seated 5511 (C511 KBT). (K. A. Jenkinson)

Two of the Optare bodies built on Leyland Olympian chassis for West Yorkshire PTE in December 1985 were convertible open-toppers. One of these – after its sale to Transdev York – 4007 (C147 KBT) is seen here in its home city operating a CitySightseeing tour on 8 August 2008. (K. A. Jenkinson)

Among the last Leyland Olympians to be bodied by Optare, E964 PME was new as a conventional double-decker in April 1988 and intended for Maidstone Borough Transport. Instead it was purchased by London Cityrama, who later converted it to part open-top. (Author's collection)

One of fifteen Optare-converted Freight Rover Sherpa 350Ds purchased by Yorkshire Rider, D712 HUA, which was new in August 1986, is seen here after its sale to Fishwick, Leyland, who numbered it M4. (K. S. E. Till)

Another Freight Rover Sherpa 350D to be converted to a sixteen-seater by Optare was C466 EWR, which was supplied new to Abbott of Workington in June 1986. (B. K. Pritchard)

Built in May 1990 for welfare duties with Leeds City Council, Optare-bodied Renault S56 G702 NUB had nine seats, and doors and a wheelchair lift in its rear bulkhead. It is seen here after being sold as a traveller's home. (Traveller Homes)

One of fifteen Leyland Cubs bodied by Optare for West Yorkshire PTE, 1810 (C810 KBT), which was new in April 1986, is seen at Bradford Interchange operating the city's Shop Hopper service, for which it is branded. (K. A. Jenkinson)

In 1986 Leeds City Council purchased two vans bodied by Optare on Ford R1115 chassis, both of which carried an Olympian front panel. D170 LWR, seen here, was new in September of that year. (Author's collection)

Supplied new to Cleveland Ambulance Service in January 1988, Optare-converted Renault Master E308 MVN had eight seats, and incorporated a wheelchair lift in its rear bulkhead. Here it is pictured after its sale for use as a mobile home. (Author's collection)

Amongst the ten Optare-bodied Leyland Olympians supplied to Reading Transport in the summer of 1988, seven were built to dual-door configuration, including 12 (E912 DRD), which is seen here attending a rally when new. (B. Newsome collection)

Three of the ten Optare-bodied Leyland Olympians purchased by Reading Transport in 1988 were coach-seated for use on its longer distance services. One of these, immaculately presented 86 (F86MJH), is seen here wearing its owner's Goldline livery. (K. A. Jenkinson)

Intended for Maidstone Borough Transport, but instead purchased new by London Cityrama in April 1988, E963 PME, which was the last Leyland Olympian to be bodied by Optare, is seen here after being sold to Gloucestershire independent Westward Travel. (Richard Covey)

Wearing Magic Rider livery, Yorkshire Rider's coach-seated Optare CityPacer-bodied VW LT55 1700 (D901 MWR) is seen here when new in April 1987. (K. A. Jenkinson)

Twenty-three-seat Optare CityPacer-bodied VW LT55 (F936 AWW) is pictured here with its original owner, Bristol-based Arrowfleet, to whom it was supplied new in August 1988. (K. A. Jenkinson)

New to VAG Commercial Vehicles, Swindon (set up by Volkswagen and Audi), in September 1986, coach-seated Optare CityPacer-bodied VW LT55 demonstrator D66 PHR is seen here displaying InterCityPacer lettering on its side panels. (B. Newsome's collection)

This view of Leeds City Council's May 1988 VW LT55 thirteen-seat welfare-bodied Optare CityPacer E690 KCP clearly shows its rear bulkhead doors, hidden behind which was a wheelchair lift. (K. A. Jenkinson)

The first buses to be exported by Optare were two left-hand drive VW LT55 CityPacers which were sold to NZH, Holland, in September 1987. One of the pair, 850 (BZ-06-HK), is seen here on a promotional duty in its new home, decorated with flowers. (Author's collection)

Optare's StarRider was built on a Mercedes Benz 811D chassis and made its debut in 1987. Here, suitably lettered thirty-three-seat demonstrator F479 FUA is seen at the Bus & Coach Show at the NEC, Birmingham, on 20 October 1989. (K. A. Jenkinson)

Amongst the first Optare StarRiders to be built was Yorkshire Rider's 2001 (E201 PWY), which was new in September 1987. Here it is seen in Forster Square, Bradford, proudly displaying its model identity on its side panels. (K. A. Jenkinson)

Berks Bucks twenty-six-seat Optare StarRider 202 (F532 NRD), adorned with a Busy Bee fleet name, was new to the company in November 1988 and is seen here at its Reading depot. In 2000 it was exported and is believed to have been purchased by a Kazakhstan owner who converted it to left-hand drive and fitted a door on the UK offside. (K. A. Jenkinson)

Standing outside Optare's Crossgates, Leeds, factory on 8 September 1991 is CityPacer-bodied VW LT55 demonstrator H847 UUA and West Midlands Travel MCW Metrobus 3107 (G107 FJW). The latter was being examined in conjunction with the design of Optare's new Spectra-bodied DAF DB250. (K. A. Jenkinson)

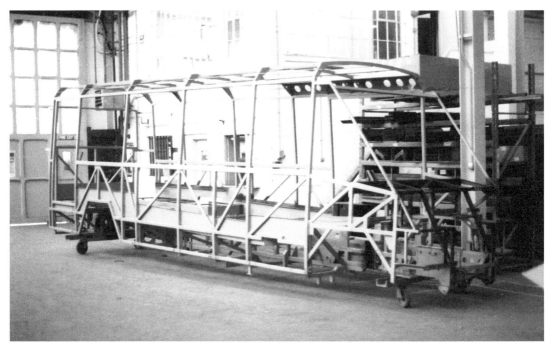

Seen at Optare's Crossgates, Leeds, factory on 16 March 1995, while under construction, is the body frame for a MetroRider integral minibus. (K. A. Jenkinson)

After gaining its mechanical units and receiving its panelling, work continues on the completion of a Blackburn Transport MetroRider, also seen here in Optare's Crossgates, Leeds, factory on 16 March 1995. (K. A. Jenkinson)

Resting in the outdoor display area at the Bus & Coach Show at the NEC, Birmingham, on 6 October 1993, is new twenty-five-seat Optare MR13 MetroRider demonstrator L735 MWW. After serving with several different operators after its sale by Optare, it was finally scrapped in 2006. (K. A. Jenkinson)

Seen in Southampton, in May 1994, is Wilts & Dorset 2508 (J508 RPR), a thirty-one-seat Optare MR05 MetroRider, which began life in June 1992 and was ultimately scrapped in 2006. (F. W. York)

Two of Arriva Durham County's Optare MetroRiders stand side by side in Darlington on 30 May 2007. On the left is thirty-one-seat MR15 2705 (R705 MHN), which was new in November 1997, while standing alongside it is twenty-five-seat MR35 2616 (P616 FHN), which had entered service a year earlier in November 1996. (K. A. Jenkinson)

New to Blackpool Transport in October 1996, twenty-five-seat Optare MR37 MetroRider P502 UFR remained in the Lancashire resort after its sale to ClassicBus North West, with whom it is seen here. (M. H. A. Flynn)

Pictured while being operated by Stagecoach Oxford is 804 (L804 HJO), which was new in November 1993 and was one of four eighteen-seat electric-powered Optare MetroRiders which were trialled in the city. (Malcolm Crowe)

Seen in Cambridge, on its first day in service, operating the free city centre shuttle in June 1996, is Stagecoach Cambus's gas-powered twenty-nine-seat Optare MR17 MetroRider 81 (GAZ 4381), which is followed by sister bus 82 (GAZ 4382). (K. A. Jenkinson)

Starting life in March 1993 with London Buses, twenty-six-seat Optare MR03 MetroRider MRL226 (K426 HWY) is seen in 2005 after being sold to Hamilton City Buses in New Zealand, by whom it was registered YY 7450 and given fleet number 91. (Author's collection)

Pictured at a bus and coach show at Donnington on 25 October 1990 is H389 SYG, a twenty-six-seat Optare-bodied Mercedes Benz 811D demonstrator. (K. A. Jenkinson)

Built in February 1989 as a demonstrator for DAF Bus, Thame, and carrying lettering on its side panels that leaves no doubt as to its mechanical pedigree, Optare Delta-bodied DAF SB220 F372 KBW is seen here in Harrogate while being trialled by West Yorkshire Road Car Co. (W. Counter)

In April 1989, Optare also had a Delta demonstrator in the form of DAF SB220 F792 DWT, which is seen here while being evaluated by Maidstone & District. Across the top of its windscreen it proudly displays that it was awarded the accolade 'Bus of the Year 1989', while on its side panels it states that it is an Optare Delta. (Author's collection)

Reading Transport was an early supporter of Optare products and purchased ten Delta-bodied DAF SB220s in the autumn of 1989. Here, 503 (G503 XBL) is seen when new in October of that year. (K. A. Jenkinson)

Displayed at the Bus & Coach Show at the NEC, Birmingham, in 1990, is thirty-six-seat dual-door Optare Delta-DAF SB220 demonstrator G684 KNW, which was new in May of that year and gave sixteen years of use before ultimately being scrapped in 2006. (K. A. Jenkinson)

Supplied new, via Optare, to Bennett, Chieveley, in May 1991, United Bus Bova Futura H13 OVA ultimately passed, in March 1999, to J. A. K. Travel, Bradford, with whom it is seen here still wearing the livery of its previous owner, Stanhope-based Weardale Motor Services. (K. A. Jenkinson)

Lined up at Optare's former Autobus Classique Hellaby plant on 9 September 2000 are First PMT Optare Solo M850 75 (W475 SVT), Optare Solo M850 demonstrator W427 CWX, Sheffield Community Transport United Bus Bova Futura P688 AUG, and MK Metro Optare Solo M920 17 (X417 BBD). (K. A. Jenkinson)

Under construction in Optare's
Crossgates, Leeds, factory on
16 March 1995 for R & I Tours,
London, is Vecta-bodied MAN
11.190 249 (M507 ALP).
(K. A. Jenkinson)

One of the 130 Optare Vecta-bodied MAN 11.190s built between April 1991 and January 1997,
Hulley of Baslow's M803 PRA began life with Trent in November 1994. (B.Newsome)

Supplied new to Scottish independent Hutchison, Overtown, in March 1994, Optare Vecta-bodied MAN 11.190 L106 YGD stayed north of the border after being acquired by Moffat & Williamson, Glenrothes, with whom it is seen here. (B. Newsome)

Amongst the buses donated to the first Asia Bus Response, following the December 2004 tsunami disaster in Sri Lanka and Indonesia, were three of Trent Barton's Optare Vecta-bodied MAN 11.190s, two of which – M807 PRA and M810 PRA – are seen here awaiting shipment to their new home in June 2005. (F. W. York)

Optare Spectra-bodied DAF DB250 demonstrator K170 FYG, which was new in August 1992, is pictured here being evaluated by Brighton Buses in April 1993. It was later sold to Reading Buses, and thence to Brightbus, North Anston, with whom it served until 2014. (K. A. Jenkinson)

New to London Buses in September 1992 numbered SP1, Optare Spectra-bodied DAF DB250 K301 FYG is seen here later in life after joining Go-Ahead Northern as its 3834. It ended its days with Brightbus at North Anston. (A. Blagburn)

Fitted from new with tree guards around its upper deck front bulkhead windows, Reading Buses low-floor Optare Spectra-bodied DAF DB250 729 (YJ03 UML) proudly displays Low Rider lettering on its lower side panels. (Author's collection)

Built as a mobile display unit for the Ministry of Defence in March 2003, Optare Spectra-bodied DAF DB250 WA03 WXZ was constructed to dual-door configuration. Later, after its sale to CCTV Direct, with whom it continued life as a display vehicle, it was re-registered YX03 HAH. (Author's collection)

One of only fifty-four Sigma-bodied Dennis Lance buses built by Optare, Stagecoach-owned Newcastle Busways 1204 (M204 DRG), which was new in September 1994, is pictured here in Newcastle-upon-Tyne in December 1996. (K. A. Jenkinson)

Starting life with Trent in November 1995 registered N364 VRC, Optare Sigma-bodied Dennis Lance TUI 8529 is seen here in November 2016 after its acquisition by Reddins, an operator situated at Muff, on the border between Ulster and Eire. (Paul Savage)

Seen under construction at Optare's Crossgates, Leeds, factory on 16 March 1995 is a Prisma-bodied Mercedes Benz O405 destined for Grampian Regional Transport as its 521 (M521 RSS). (K. A. Jenkinson)

Awaiting its passengers in Rochdale bus station on 3 June 2003 is First Manchester's Optare Prisma-bodied Mercedes Benz O405 60430 (R524 RSS), which had started life with Grampian Regional Transport in July 1995. (M. H. A. Flynn)

Seen on 15 September 2015, shortly after being acquired for preservation, is ex-Red Kite, St Helens, Optare Prisma-bodied Mercedes Benz 0405 TIL 7902, which was new to Tillingbourne, Cranleigh, in September 1997, registered R202 YOR. (K. A. Jenkinson)

Originally registered N990 FWT when new to Baildon Motors, Guiseley, in February 1996, Autobus Classique Nouvelle-bodied Mercedes Benz 814D YIL 2271 is seen here under the ownership of Goodyear, Mapplewell. (M. H. A. Flynn)

Starting life with Cropper, Kirkstall, Leeds, in April 1999, thirty-three-seat Autobus Classique Nouvelle 2-bodied Mercedes Benz 0814D T56 RJL is seen here after joining Shuttle Buses, Kilwinning. (B. Newsome)

Left-hand drive Autobus Classique Nouvelle 2-bodied Mercedes Benz 814D LLB 31093 is pictured here in Lublin, Poland, on a snowy winter's day in 2010. (Author's collection)

Originating with Horseman, Reading, in October 1997, nineteen-coach-seated, air-conditioned, Autobus Classique-bodied Mercedes Benz 312D R791 WOY was captured through the lens after its sale to Bankfoot Buses, Perth. (Author's collection)

Built in November 1995 as an Optare demonstrator, thirty-four-seat Excel L1000 prototype N330 EUG is seen here when new, proudly adorned with 'The Revolutionary Excel' lettering on its side panels. (Author's collection)

New to Stockton Borough Council in September 1999 as a twenty-seat bus registered V824 DHN, and now operated by Leydons Coaches, Swanlinbar, Co. Cavan, Eire, is Optare Excel L1000 99-CN-6018, seen here on the 930 service to Enniskillen. (Paul Savage)

Starting life in April 1997 with Harris Bus, West Thurrock, thirty-five-seat Optare Excel L1070 P332 NHJ is pictured here at Stratford bus station after passing to East London Buses. (K. A. Jenkinson)

Trent took a great liking to the Optare Excel and purchased 112 examples between September 1998 and March 2001. Here, forty-six-seat L1150 208 (V208 ENU), which was new in February 2000, is seen in Stockport bus station in April 2006, operating Skyline service 199 from Buxton to Manchester Airport, for which it is branded. (M. H. A. Flynn)

Seen in the bowels of Holyhead Port on 30 April 2017, Stena Line's dual-door Optare Excel L1150 T785 KNW, which also had a centre door on its offside, began life at London's Heathrow airport in June 1999 with Concord Express. (Paul Savage)

Former Reading Transport thirty-nine-seat Optare Excel L1080 X964 BPA is seen here in the fleet of the now defunct North Wales independent Express Motors, who re-registered it EXI 790. (M. H. A. Flynn)

Seen when new in September 2008, and marketed in the UK by Optare, is Ferqui Soroco-bodied Mercedes Benz Sprinter YX58 AUA. (Optare)

Thirty-five-seat Ferqui Solera-bodied Mercedes Benz Atego 1223L YX06 AXT, with its passenger entrance door aft of the front axle, is pictured when new to McNee, Ratho Station, in April 2006. (Optare)

Seen when new in 2010 is a Spanish-built Ferqui SoleraHD-bodied Mercedes Benz 1324L, its door forward of the front axle, which, as can be seen from its registration number plate, was being marketed by Optare. (Optare)

New in July 2008 to Walsh, Halifax, twenty-three-seat Optare M710SE slimline Solo MX08 DFZ is seen here in Glasgow, in May 2019, after being sold to Paisley independent Key Coaches. (D. W. Rhodes)

One of a pair of slimline Optare Solo M710SEs, purchased new in August 2008 by Leeds Bradford airport for operation on its long-stay car park shuttle service, YJ08 PGK only had seating for sixteen passengers to allow extra luggage racking to be accommodated. (K. A. Jenkinson)

Operated when new, in April 2006, by First Bradford on behalf of West Yorkshire Metro, Optare Solo M780 53824 (YJ06 FYS) is seen resting in Bradford Interchange on 4 April 2017, after being transferred to local independent operator TLC. (K. A. Jenkinson)

Collecting its passengers in Ripon bus station, on 25 September 2013, is now defunct Eddie Brown of Thorp Arch's thirty-five-seat Optare Solo M990 KX04 HPU, which began life with Landylines, Greenham, in May 2004. (K. A. Jenkinson)

Purchased new by Brylaine, Boston, in March 2005, is thirty-seven-seat Optare Solo M950 YJ05 JXK, pictured here in Boston bus station. (M. H. A. Flynn)

Seen in Manchester, operating one of the free city centre Metro Shuttle services, is First Manchester 40335 (ML02 OGE), a twenty-six-seat Optare Solo M850 which was new in July 2002. (M. H. A. Flynn)

Having been sold by McEwan, Amisfield, to M Travel, Glasshoughton, thirty-seven-seat Optare Solo M1020 MX55 BXP, seen passing through City Square, Leeds, en route to its new owner on 8 January 2014, had begun life with Supertravel, Speke, in November 2005. (K. A. Jenkinson)

Stagecoach Lincolnshire's biomethane-powered Optare Solo M920 47273 (FX04 WFT), which was new in April 2004, is seen here at Lincoln bus station. (Author's collection)

One of four Optare Solo M850s supplied in 2002 to Age Concern for silver surfers' computer training, FG02 BTX had seating for eight people and was fitted with an on-board toilet. (B. Newsome collection)

Seen in Preston's iconic bus station, showing their front and rear profiles, are Stagecoach Lancashire Optare Solo M880s 47470 (PX07 GZU) and 47479 (PX07 HBA), which were new in June 2007 and July 2007 respectively. (K. A. Jenkinson)

Purchased new by Billund Airport, Denmark, in March 2007, was left-hand drive Optare Solo M880L UZ 90 233, which unusually had a centre door. (Author's collection)

Built in January 2008 as a promotional vehicle for Macmillan Cancer Support, Optare Solo M920 YJ57 EHK, which had a centre rather than front door, is seen here performing its duties in Stockport. (Author's collection)

Built in September 2003 as an overseas demonstrator, dual-door, left-hand drive Optare Solo M920L YN53 SVF displays 'New Euro Solo' lettering across its side windows. (Optare)

BBG, Eberswalde, Germany's, thirty-seat dual-door, left-hand drive Optare Solo M1020L 166 (BAR FR 810), which was new in December 2008, makes its way along a cobbled street in its home surroundings. (Author's collection)

Seen in Belfast, on 3 December 2017, operating a park & ride service, for which it carries branding, is Translink Metro twenty-six-seat Optare Solo M850, 1828 (SCZ 1848), which was new in May 2003. (Paul Savage)

Seen in service with Arriva Malta, twenty-nine-seat hybrid Optare Solo M880H BUS 276, which was new in August 2011, shows off its full-depth centre emergency exit, all standard Solos having this positioned after the rear axle. (Paul Emery)

Fitted with a large, single-piece front door, 6061 (BX-XB-08) is one of seven twenty-one-seat, left-hand drive Optare Solo M810Ls supplied to Arriva Nederland in December 2010. (Author's collection)

Seen at Leeds Bradford airport at the launch of its contract for the service to Leeds in November 2004 is Aztecbird, Steeton's, new twenty-nine-seat Optare Solo M1020 YJ54 BVA, which was painted in West Yorkshire PTE's Metro Connect livery with added branding for the 737 service. (K. A. Jenkinson)

Built in April 2009 as an Optare demonstrator and seen here with incorrect registration number YJ60 EZR (which should read YJ09 EZR), this twenty-five-seat M880EV was its manufacturer's prototype electric Solo. (Optare)

Seen in Liverpool is YJ12 GXA, a twenty-three-seat hybrid Optare Solo M810H with front-mounted roof pod. It was supplied new to independent Cumfybus in April 2012. (M. H. A. Flynn)

Built at Optare's Crossgates, Leeds, factory as a prototype for NABI, Hungary, is this thirty-three-seat, dual-door, left-hand drive Excel L1189L, which was caught on camera outside Optare's Autobus Classique premises, at Hellaby, on 9 September 2000. (K. A. Jenkinson)

Pictured in Hungary, dual-door NABI 700SE demonstrator JDY 594, which was based on Optare's Excel model but built on a Scania L94UB chassis, was one of thirteen built at NABI's new Kaposvar factory in 2002/3. (Optare NABI)

Seen here in Kaposvar, IDU 560 was a three-door NABI 700SE built on a Scania L94UB chassis in May 2002 and was one of seven operated by Kaposvári Tomegközlekedési. (Author's collection)

One of seventy left-hand drive NABI 30-LFNs – badge engineered Optare Solos – built in Budapest for Miami Dade Transit, USA. 03357 was new in 2003. (Author's collection)

Seen in the confines of NABI's Budapest factory on 6 May 2005 is the prototype fibreglass-constructed Compobus which was being used as a test bed for the new model. (K. A. Jenkinson)

Mounted on a flat platform, the body frame of the front module of a 60-BRT bendy bus is seen here being pushed by hand, on rails, across NABI's Budapest factory on 6 May 2005. (K. A. Jenkinson)

Seen at NABI's Budapest factory on 6 May 2005, ready for shipping to NABI's Anniston, Alabama, USA, plant for finishing, is the unglazed shell of a 60-BRT bendy bus destined for operation in Las Vegas. (K. A. Jenkinson)

One of the NABI 60-BRTs built in Budapest and finished in Anniston, Alabama, USA, is seen here in service with Los Angeles Metro Rapid in the USA. (Optare NABI)

New in June 2004, London Borough of Richmond's sixteen-seat Optare Alero YN04 YBE has a plain front roof dome and lacks a destination box. (Optare)

Resting in Wrexham bus station while operated by Arriva North West & Wales, and showing its wide outward-opening doors, is Optare Alero 619 (YN04 XZH), which was new in May 2004 to Sheffield Community Transport. (Wikimedia)

Built in October 2001 as a sixteen-seat Alero bus for Hackney Community Transport and registered YL51 XCR, this was later re-registered XIL 8947 before being converted, in 2004, into a service van for Optare's Unitec division, with whom it is seen here. (Optare)

Built by Spanish coachbuilder Ferqui on a Fiat Ducato chassis, this Bonito mini coach began life as a demonstrator in 2012 and is seen here proudly displaying an Optare logo on its front grille. (Optare)

Of the twenty-three Agora Line-bodied Irisbus single-deckers completed by Optare, fourteen were purchased by Norfolk County Council for use on its Norwich Park & Ride services, upon which 7136 (OY5RFF), which was new in September 2003, is seen here. (D. W. Rhodes)

Harlow independent SM Coaches purchased its solitary Optare-Irisbus Angora Line, EU06 KHK, when it was new in May 2006. Here it is seen laying over between duties in its hometown bus station. (John Podgorski)

One of five dual-door, hydrogen-powered Optare Tempo X1060Hs supplied to Metroline, London, early in 2009, is seen here on display at the Bus & Coach Show at the NEC, Birmingham, on 5 November 2008. (K. A. Jenkinson)

Seen wearing SPT (Strathclyde Partnership for Transport) livery is Henderson of Hamilton's thirty-four-seat Optare Tempo X1060 YJ06 YSH. (Optare)

Displaying 'xprss' branding for the service between Nottingham and Bingham, Trent Barton Optare Tempo X1200 301 (FD54 JXZ) is seen here awaiting its passengers in Nottingham on 24 April 2009. (K. A. Jenkinson)

Purchased new in November 2006 by Leeds Bradford Airport, for airside duties, is this unregistered Optare Tempo X1200 which seated twenty-five passengers and had dual doors on both sides of its body. (Optare)

This left-hand drive, dual-door Optare Tempo X1200 demonstrator, which was new in 2007, is seen here carrying a Danish registration mark, but was displaying Schipol (Amsterdam) on its destination screens. (Optare)

Purchased new by Courtney, Bracknell, forty-seven-seat Optare Tempo X1060s YJ10 EXT and YJ10 EXS are seen here at their launch at Chineham Park in April 2010. (Optare)

New in April 2010, Centrebus's thirty-eight-seat Optare Tempo X1130 773 (YJ10 EZF) is seen here approaching Halifax bus station at the end of its journey from Midgley, on 23 October 2010. (K. A. Jenkinson)

Displayed at the 2007 Bus & Coach Show at the NEC, Birmingham, is Optare-marketed, Ferqui-built Mercedes Benz 0816D Toro demonstrator YX57 BZP. (K. A. Jenkinson)

New in 2007 for a German customer is this Ferqui Rapido-bodied Iveco, which was also marketed in the UK by Optare. (Author's collection)

Seen under construction at Optare's Sherburn-in-Elmet factory, in September 2018, are two Versa V1170s for Transdev Blazefield Rosso. (Optare)

Branded for the service to George Best Belfast City Airport, and seen in August 2016, is Translink Metro forty-three-seat Optare Versa V1170 1801 (TFZ 8801), which was new in October 2014. (Paul Savage)

Built to dual-door configuration with twenty-five seats, one of Manchester Airport's fourteen Optare Versa V1170s, which were purchased new in February and April 2015, YJ15 AWY, is pictured here undertaking a staff shuttle duty, within the airport's confines, in September of that year. (M. H. A. Flynn)

Resting in the yard of Stagecoach Manchester's Wigan depot, in February 2019, are four fifty-seven-seat diesel-electric hybrid Optare Versa V1210Hs which were new in April 2012 and are operated on school bus duties on behalf of Transport for Greater Manchester. (K. S. E. Till)

Owned by NCP Services (Challenger), twenty-seven-seat dual-door Optare Versa V1040 OVL62 (YJ09 EYZ) is seen here en route to East Acton on TfL route 283 in July 2009, when only four months old. (John Podgorski)

Displayed at the Bus & Coach Show at the NEC, Birmingham, on 7 November 2018, is thirty-four-seat Optare Versa V1170xFE demonstrator OP07 ARE. (Paul Savage)

Posed for the camera standing near Optare's Sherburn-in-Elmet factory in 2007 are three Optare demonstrators: Tempo X1200 YJ06F ZK, Versa YJ56 ATF, and original-style Solo YJ56 ATE, the latter two of which are displaying fictitious registration marks. (Optare)

At the 2011 Bus & Coach Show at the NEC, Birmingham, Optare displayed this twenty-eight-seat SoloSR M890, YJ11 OJK, which was initially used by its manufacturer as a demonstrator. (K. A. Jenkinson)

Resting in Harrogate bus station, on 23 October 2014, is Transdev Harrogate & District thirty-one-seat electric Optare Solo M925EV 999 (YJ14 BCK) which, at the time, was only seven months old. (K. A. Jenkinson)

The only Optare SoloSR to be supplied to Hong Kong was nineteen-seat M7900SE VF 7558, which was purchased by AMS Public Transport in January 2018. (Optare)

This rear view of Stanley Travel's (Oxhill) twenty-three-seat Optare SoloSR M710SE R2 STX, which was new in June 2015, shows the alternative styling being offered with a revised bumper and lights. (Optare)

Awaiting its passengers at Leeds Bradford Airport, on 26 June 2017, is the Keighley Bus Company's thirty-four-seat Optare Solo M9950SR 153 (YJ16 DVG), which was new in June 2016. (K. A. Jenkinson)

Strathclyde PTE-owned nineteen-seat Optare SoloSR M720SE YD63 UZO, which began life in December 2013, is seen here being operated on Strathclyde's behalf by McColls, Dumbarton. (D. W. Rhodes)

One of 110 twenty-five-seat right-hand drive Optare SoloSR M890s supplied to MyCiti, Cape Town, South Africa, between July 2012 and August 2013, CA 973 458, like all its sisters, had a front nearside and centre offside door. (Optare)

Leaving Buchanan bus station, Glasgow, at the start of its journey to Lanark, is Stuarts (Carluke) twenty-nine-seat Optare Solo M9250SR YJ66 AOS, which its owner purchased new in September 2016. (D. W. Rhodes)

New in October 2013, Ross Travel of Featherstone's thirty-six-seat Optare SoloSR M960, YD63 UZH, is seen here at Castleford bus station on the 146 service to Pontefract. (K. A. Jenkinson)

Displayed at the Bus & Coach Show at the NEC, Birmingham, in October 2015, this Optare SoloSR proudly displays 'I am a low carbon bus' lettering on its side panels. (K. A. Jenkinson)

Joining the twenty-nine Optare Solo M9700SRs supplied to CT Plus, Jersey, in November 2012 were a pair of twenty-five-seat M8500SRs, which took up their duties in October 2017. One of the latter, 334 (J138090), is seen here shortly after entering service. (Libertybus)

Seen on display at the Bus & Coach Show at the NEC, Birmingham, in November 2017, is slim line Optare Solo M7800SR YJ67 GEK, which started life as a demonstrator for its manufacturer. Although the lettering on its side windows shows its carrying capacity to be thirty-six passengers, only twenty-four were seated, the remaining twelve being standees. (K. A. Jenkinson)

Built in July 2013 as a thirty-one-seat all-electric Optare Solo M890EV demonstrator and registered YJ13 HKY, after undergoing some re-engineering it was re-registered OP02 ARE in 2018 and is seen here being evaluated by Go Coach Hire, Sevenoaks. (Optare)

Pictured here is the battery pack fitted to Optare's electrically powered Versa V1110EVs. (Optare)

Displaying 'Inverness Electricity' on its side windows, to leave passengers no doubt as to its propulsion, is Stagecoach in the Highlands twenty-nine-seat Optare SoloSR M890EV 48904 (YJ15 AWH), which was new in March 2015, and is seen here in its home city. (Murdoch Currie)

Seen in Utrecht is Dutch operator Qbuzz of Amersfoort's left-hand drive, thirty-seven-seat, dual-door, electrically propelled Optare SoloSR M995EV 4301 (54-BDJ-9), which was new in January 2014. (Author's collection)

Standing outside Optare's Sherburn-in-Elmet factory in January 2012, awaiting delivery to First Manchester, is twenty-seven-seat, diesel-electric hybrid SoloSR M890H 59009 (YJ61 JDO). (Optare)

New to Kent County Council in October 2008, forty-three-seat Optare Esteem-bodied Volvo B7RLE PO58 KPX, which was built to the erstwhile East Lancs Coachbuilders design, is seen here in Canterbury operating a park & ride service. (D. W. Rhodes)

Built by Optare to East Lancs Esteem design, Go-Ahead London General's dual-door, twenty-nine-seat SOE22 (LX09 AZF), on an AlexanderDennis Enviro200 chassis, was new in June 2009 and was one of the last Esteems to be built. (D. W. Rhodes)

One of the first bodies to be built under Optare ownership of the former East Lancs factory in Blackburn was Nottingham City Transport Scania N270UD 947 (YN08 MSV), which was new in July 2008, and had an East Lancs-designed OmniDekka body. (M. H. A. Flynn)

Although it has a high quality paint finish which has caused numerous reflections, Optare's new Rapta double-decker, seen here at the November 2008 Bus & Coach Show at the NEC, Birmingham, with no interior fittings, was widely spurned by operators, and as a consequence was never completed. Instead it was abandoned, as seen in the next photograph. (Malcolm Crowe)

Intended as Optare's new double-decker, the Rapta was an integrally constructed model which made its debut at the November 2008 Bus & Coach Show at the NEC, Birmingham. After being rejected by operators, the sole prototype, which was never internally equipped, is seen here before ultimately being dismantled. (Optare)

Also exhibited at the November 2008 Bus & Coach Show was Optare's new Solo+, which was planned as a replacement for the existing Solo range. Like the Rapta, it too was disliked by operators, with the result that it was immediately abandoned. Here, the only Solo+ to be built and internally fitted is seen at the show wearing an uninspiring silver-grey livery. (K. A. Jenkinson)

Using East Lancs Olympus body styling and built in December 2012 as the prototype for Optare's Metrodecker, designated the 01030 model, YJ62 FNR (originally registered in the UK) was later sold to Lepeirks Travel, Gozo (Malta), where it is seen here. It was locally registered HPY 003 after being converted to open-top format. (Author's collection)

Built at Blackburn by Optare, to East Lancs Olympus design, Johnsons (Henley-in-Arden) Scania N230UD PN09 ENJ, which was new in March 2009, is seen here in Birmingham city centre branded for the X20 service to Stratford-on-Avon. (K. A. Jenkinson)

Originally registered D10 SLT when new to Green Triangle, Atherton, in April 2010, this Blackburn-built Optare Olympus-bodied Scania N230UD is seen here after its sale to Midland Classic, Burton-upon-Trent, who numbered it 51 and re-registered it JB10 MCL. (R. G. Pope)

Constructed at Blackburn on a tri-axle Volvo B9TL chassis, this 100 coach-seated Optare Olympus was supplied new to Soul, Olney, in September 2008. (Optare)

Branded for the Purbeck Breezer service, and seen at Swanage, is Wilts & Dorset 1405 (HF09 FVY), an open-top Blackburn-built Optare Visionaire-bodied Scania N230UD, which was based on the East Lancs Olympus, and was new in August 2009. (M. H. A. Flynn)

Crossing Westminster Bridge, London, is sightseeing operator Big Bus's part open-top Optare
Visionaire-bodied tri-axle Volvo B9TL DA321 (PN10 FOC), which began life in March 2010.
(Big Bus)

Displayed at the November 2016 Bus & Coach Show at the NEC, Birmingham, is an all-electric
Optare MetroCity EV extra range V1080MC painted in Transport for London livery.
(K. A. Jenkinson)

Also shown at the 2016 Bus & Coach Show was Optare MetroCity XFE V1152MC YJ17 FXE, which was later employed as a demonstrator. (K. A. Jenkinson)

Seen at Birmingham airport operating a shuttle service to an off-site car park on 3 November 2016 is Optare MetroCity V1010MC YJ65 EPY, which was new in September 2015 to APH, Sharston. (K. A. Jenkinson)

Fitted with dual-purpose seating for forty passengers and painted in a dedicated livery for the Traws Cymru services, this is Richards' (Cardigan) Optare MetroCity V1152MC YJ15 AWP, which began life in April 2015. (M. H. A. Flynn)

Pictured operating Manchester's city centre free Metro Shuttle service is First Manchester twenty-eight-seat Optare Versa V970H hybrid 49112 (YJ60 KDX), which made its debut in November 2010. (M. H. A. Flynn)

Thirty-two-seat all-electric Optare Versa V1040EV YD63 VAE was new in December 2013 and numbered 941 by Nottingham Community Transport, who used it on its Medilink service, for which it carried appropriate branding. (Optare)

Leaving Optare's Sherburn-in-Elmet factory in April 2018, at the start of its long journey across the world to New Zealand, where it was to be operated by the Transit Group, is thirty-three-seat dual-door Versa MetroCity V1080MC 3101 (LHG 22). (Optare)

Built as a demonstrator, the first Optare Metrodecker MD1114 to enter service was YJ65 EPU, which made its debut in September 2015 and is seen here displayed at the October 2015 Bus & Coach Show at the NEC, Birmingham, painted in Yorkshire Tiger livery. (K. A. Jenkinson)

Seen when new in August 2017, before being registered YJ17 FXX and evaluated by First York, is the prototype electric-powered, dual-door, Optare Metrodecker MD1050 demonstrator. (Optare)

Promoting the fact on its destination indicator that it is 100 per cent electric is Metroline, London, dual-door Optare Metrodecker MD1050EV OME2650 (YJ19 HVA), which was new in May 2019 and is seen here, two months later, at an event at its owner's Potters Bar garage. (Nigel Eadon-Clarke)

Given new frontal styling, and built in March 2012 as an Optare demonstrator, YJ12 GYK was a forty-one-seat Tempo X1200SR, and is seen here in its original livery. (Optare)

Also showing the revised frontal appearance of Optare's Tempo model is trentbarton's X1200SR 335 (YJ12 GWU), which was new in July 2012 and is seen here wearing a branded livery for the i4 service between Sandiacre and Nottingham. (Optare)

The only triple-door Optare Tempo to be supplied to a UK customer is twenty-nine-seat X1260SR YJ17 FYE, which was purchased by Manchester Airport in May 2017 and is seen here operating a staff shuttle duty. (Author's collection)

First York all-electric Optare Versa V1110EV 49911 (YJ15 AYN) is seen here being recharged at its Poppleton Bar Park & Ride terminus. (Optare)

A sizeable number of Optare Solos have been exported to Australia, including a pair of thirty-seat M995SRs which were purchased by Gold Bus, Ballarat, Victoria, in May 2014. Fitted with heavy front bumpers, BS00 OU, like its sister, was acquired for school transport duties. (Author's collection)

Seen on UK trade plates, heading southbound along the A1M near Ferrybridge on the first part of its journey to Dubai on 29 May 2019, is this brand new Optare Solo M8500SR, one of a number purchased by the Emirate's Roads and Transport Authority. (Rick Ward)

Two ex-Trent Optare Deltas that were exported to Falklands Islands Tours and Travel are seen here in May 2019, several years after their operational lives had ended. (Tim Cotter)

New to Nottingham City Transport in January 2002 and later serving with Goodwins, Eccles, Optare Excel L1180 WEZ 7837, originally FD51 EYU, ended its life as a bus banger racer at Buxton Raceway where it is seen here, complete with a seat belt on the driver's seat, on 17 April 2017. (Author's collection)

One of five twenty-one-seat, dual-door, left-hand drive Optare Solo M880Ls, purchased new by DAN Public Transportation Co., Tel Aviv, Israel, in April 2010, 5306 is seen here in January 2019, with its centre door having been filled in, relegated to living accommodation after its passenger-carrying days had ended. (Author's collection)

Proudly proclaiming that it is 100 per cent electric, on delivery from Optare's Sherburn-in-Elmet factory to its new London owner, Metroline, dual-door Metrodecker MD1050EV OME2659 (YJ19 HVM) heads southbound on the A1M on 29 July 2019. (Rick Ward)

A partly built Versa stands in the yard of Optare's Crossgates, Leeds, factory a few days after its closure in October 2011. (Author's collection)

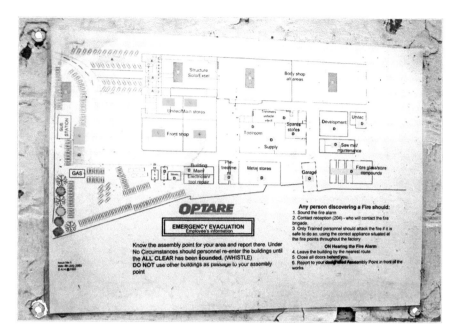

Seen here is a floor and fire evacuation plan of Optare's Crossgates, Leeds, factory in its final year of production. (Author's collection)

The sad sight of the bodyshop at Optare's Crossgates, Leeds, plant in November 2011, after it had been emptied and all its equipment moved to its new factory at Sherburn-in-Elmet. (Author's collection)

Optare's custom-built factory at Sherburn-in-Elmet, to which it moved in 2011 when it vacated the former Chas H. Roe works at Crossgates, Leeds. (Optare)